Cryptocurrency Investing Guide

How To Make A Lot Of Money By Investing in Bitcoin, Ethereum, Litecoin & Ripple

David Johnson

Table of Contents

Introduction

In this book, **Cryptocurrency Investing Guide: How to Make a Lot of Money by Investing in Bitcoin, Ethereum, Litecoin & Ripple**, you'll be learning how to invest in cryptocurrencies. Here, you'll find essential information about the most popular cryptocurrencies, especially Bitcoin, Ethereum, Litecoin, and Ripple, as well as information on a list of Altcoins.

Some of the topics featured in this book are:

- The blockchain technology

- Popular cryptocurrencies (such as Bitcoin, Litecoin, Ethereum, Ripple)

- Other emerging cryptocurrencies

- How to buy cryptocurrencies

- How to trade cryptocurrencies

- How to handle cryptocurrencies

Apart from an exposure to the core concept of cryptocurrencies – how they work and what technology they're based on, you'll learn how to buy, trade, and manage cryptocurrencies. Here, you'll be learning practical steps as you build a career as a cryptocurrency investor.

If you're new to these investments, worrying about the future is not rare. But try not to worry. Sure, the subject of cryptocurrency investments can seem intimidating. Once you familiarize yourself with its concept, though, you're likely to realize otherwise.

With the rapid increase in the current prices of cryptocurrencies, it's no secret why you'd want to jump in on the bandwagon, too. Many have bet their fates in the industry and have reaped the rewards. Granted you invest wisely, you can make a lot of money with them.

Are you familiar with the Winklevoss twins? How about Tim Draper, Charlie Shrem, and Barry Silbert? You can be just like these rich guys who bravely invested in these cryptocurrencies and watched them soar in the financial markets through the years.

Thanks for downloading this book!

Chapter 1 – The Blockchain Technology

Let's say you're going to send money (in the form of five bitcoin tokens) to a friend.

If it were traditional money, you would have to go to a bank for them to process it for you. Since you need to compensate for the bank's services, this arrangement incurs transaction fees. And since banks only operate during business days, delays may be part of the deal, too.

Because these are cryptocurrencies, the service of a bank (or any other 3rd party) is unnecessary. Consequently, you eliminate the need to pay additional fees and delays.

This more affordable arrangement is possible since cryptocurrencies are not like traditional money. Their system works under the blockchain technology.

An Introduction to the Blockchain

A P2P (peer-to-peer) network powers the blockchain technology. This network assigns influential power of the same caliber to each member. So even if member #1 owns more cryptocurrencies than member #2, both members still have equal influence within the network.

An anonymous entity by the name of Satoshi Nakamoto invented the blockchain technology. From its creation in 2008 and implementation in 2009, developers worldwide have pitched in and made it the marvel that it is today.

Here are some facts about the blockchain technology:

- A beauty of the blockchain technology is its allowance for the distribution of digital information. Its design is to hold digital information, which anyone can reconcile continually. There is no single location for the blockchain technology's database; the records are easily verifiable and are made public. It is accessible to just about everyone with an internet connection.

- No one owns the blockchain technology – not the government, not a group of billionaires, not hackers. This is advantageous since a need to protect it against threats of centralized authorization doesn't exist. This also means it can serve as a transport layer, which allows the use and development of additional applications without the consent or approval of another.

- It is very secure. While it grants accessibility to everyone, it doesn't manipulate information. The transactions it records on a single block isn't modifiable retroactively without initiating modifications in all succeeding blocks and without the network's collusion.

This Is How the Blockchain Works

The blockchain works as a digital ledger. It follows an iterative process, which confirms a previous block's integrity – retracing steps to the genesis block.

Think of it as a spreadsheet. This spreadsheet is duplicated (and re-duplicated as many times) across a large network of computers, in which regular updates to the spreadsheet's contents are part of its design.

Here's a breakdown of its structure:

- First, it processes blocks. These blocks contain transactions.

  Depending on a particular cryptocurrency, blocks are processed promptly. In the case of Bitcoin, its block processing time is 10 minutes.

- Once validated, these transactions are then forwarded to a Merkle tree or a hash tree. They are hashed and encoded in the process. A processed block then establishes a link to other blocks, in which the link forms a chain of blocks.

  There are cases when the blockchain technology identifies a block that is attempting to reverse a transaction. In this scenario, this block (called orphaned block) is detached from the link.

Chapter 2 – The Power of Cryptocurrencies

Like the blockchain technology, a major upside to cryptocurrencies is their lack of reliance on a central bank or a regulatory authority. As decentralized money, they're not under the regulation of any government. So as an owner of cryptocurrencies, you need not worry about government-imposed taxes and laws. Cryptocurrencies are free when you need to transfer and to hold.

It's easier to recognize this as an upside if you compare the use of cryptocurrencies with the use of traditional currencies such as USD.

If you send USD, which is predominantly controlled by banks, you need to pay fees for a transaction to proceed. Conversely, using cryptocurrencies, which isn't controlled by any authority, is totally free.

Here's a list of top cryptocurrencies:

Bitcoin

Arguably, Bitcoin is skyrocketing in popularity as a cryptocurrency. As the 1st established cryptocurrency, it started all the fuzz with cryptocurrencies. For about $10,000 per token as of the early 2018, it has definitely gone far since its initial release in 2009.

According to notable financial analysts (including Jim Cramer at CNBC), the cryptocurrency's price has the potential to reach as much as $1 million sometime soon. Considering Bitcoin's jump in terms of market capitalization from $170 billion (September 2017) to $700 billion (January 2018) in just 4 months, this prediction is likely going in the right direction.

Strengths:

- **It is the most popular cryptocurrency.** In the hierarchy of cryptocurrencies, it owns the #1 spot. In fact, the word "Bitcoin" is probably the 1st word that comes to most people's mind when the word "cryptocurrency" is mentioned.

- **Its network owns massive computing power.** 2,046,364 (Peta) FLOPS is its computing power, which is way more than the computing power of the world's fastest supercomputer. The fastest supercomputer, known to have the top operational rate of all computers, operates as much as 93 (Peta) FLOPS. So even if a thousand supercomputers are combined, which could accumulate a computing power of 93,000 (Peta) FLOPS, Bitcoin's network is still the winner.

- **It is the most liquid cryptocurrency.** Most cryptocurrency exchanges accept Bitcoin to USD conversions. So if you decide to cash in your Bitcoin tokens, finding an exchange for this purpose isn't difficult.

  Additionally, on April 1, 2017, Japan's legislature submitted a law that recognizes bitcoin as a legal payment instrument. In this country, along with other countries such as South Korea and Canada, Bitcoin is gaining fans as a trusted and recognizable asset.

- **It is the least volatile among all cryptocurrencies.** The highly-volatile nature of cryptocurrencies is worrisome, especially to conservative investors. But Bitcoin is not nearly as high as the volatility of other cryptocurrencies.

According to the Bitcoin Volatility Index, 6.71% is the estimate of Bitcoin's weekly volatility in 2017. The volatility percentages of Ethereum and Litecoin, on the other hand, are 9.41% and 8.28%, respectively.

Weaknesses:

- **Its block processing time is 10 minutes.** Compared to the block processing times of other cryptocurrencies, this is slow. This delays the processing of large transactions.

- **It has a limited supply.** 21 million Bitcoin tokens is a lot for a single people, or even for 1,000 people. But you wouldn't say the same for all the people in the world, which is roughly 7.6 billion.

- **It lacks stability.** Its price fluctuations are worrisome. While it could reach the $10,000 mark in a short period, it could also plunge by hundreds of dollars just as quickly.

  And this high volatility makes it highly risky. Due to its unpredictability, what could be advantageous could also have disastrous results. Someone could be a bitcoin millionaire this week, only to become bankrupt by the following week. For example, its price on the Bitfinex financial market dropped to about 1/3 in just about a week's time.

Ethereum

Another popular term in the world of cryptocurrencies is Ethereum. Ethereum is a blockchain-based computing platform and its cryptocurrency component is called Ether, which is traded as ETH. It's based on a Proof of Stake algorithm.

Its creator is a math genius named Vitalik Buterin. His aim is to lower the inflation rate by about 2%, and he's doing an excellent job so far -- as can be backed by the 2,800% appreciation in the price of Ether tokens since 2015.

Google Trends reports a growth in Ethereum's search interest. Many people (especially the Swiss and Venezuelans) reveal their curiosity about it online via search engines. From its market debut on July 30, 2015, it has gone a long way and now has millions of followers. In mid-March 2017, the keyword "Ethereum" has peaked its record in search popularity.

Strengths:

- **The Ethereum network has laid out a promising roadmap for Ether.** Its network's mission is to replace server farms and be a world computer. While its mission may seem ambitious, it has proven to be capable of continuing its appreciation streak. And since it has a crystal clear vision of its future place (in 3 to 5 years), many people can identify its network's transparency, and therefore, feel confident in investing in it.

- **It is steadily increasing in value.** While it is highly-volatile just like other cryptocurrencies, it has a higher percentage of gain (compared to Bitcoin).

- **It doesn't have a fixed supply cap (maximum).** Since the Ethereum network is relatively new, the availability of Ether tokens is higher. Currently, CoinMarketCap.com reports more than 97 million Ether tokens are in circulation as of February 2018. Compared to Bitcoin's 21 million supply, this is beneficial.

- **It has its own platform.** It is, therefore, the technologically-smarter cryptocurrency compared to other digital assets such as Bitcoin and Litecoin. With Ether, you can begin implementing smart contracts.

- **It comes with democratic autonomous organizations.** Its decentralized arrangement protects you from experiencing downtime. And on top of helping you with source funding, it provides good organizational structure that can help you launch a startup. After you have financial supporters, you can begin collecting proposals, and then host a vote-casting event with regard to your next actions.

- **It aims to elevate the fundraising scene.** Its involvement in fundraisers comes with a maximum impact. Not only does it help raise funds for charitable causes; it also has its own fundraising platform called Grace Ethereum platform.

Weaknesses:

- **It has its own blockchain.** And while this can be beneficial, it is also a downside since this means it is not fully centralized. No government entity owns it. But the people behind the Ethereum network – headed by its creator – do. This means that the Ethereum Network dictates rules.

Litecoin

Then, there's Litecoin with the code LTC. Its creator, Charlie Lee, designed its algorithm using a Proof of Work scheme. It can, therefore, fight attacks involving service abuses such as spam and denial of service.

Litecoin is a lot like Bitcoin; both digital assets have similar encryption techniques. The main difference is Litecoin operates faster – a lot faster. Think of it as a lite version of Bitcoin. If Bitcoin were gold, Litecoin would be silver.

Strengths:

- **It can process a block within 2.5 minutes.** While it may currently be inferior to bitcoin's price, it is said to have more potential than bitcoin. Its block processing time is 4x than bitcoin. If you need to process 10 blocks, you only need to wait about 25 minutes with it. But if you use Bitcoin, you would need to wait more than an hour.

- **It has no concerns with block sizes.** It features a process called SegWit (Segregated Witness), which recognizes limits to block sizes and then increases these limits. It also eliminates some components of a blockchain and then increases space capacity for additional transactions to be processed.

- **It can produce a higher token supply.** 84 million Litecoin tokens are producible. According to CoinMarketCap.com, there are more than 55 million Litecoins in circulation as of February 2018.

- **It significantly reduces the risk of double spending.** With the fast block generation time, it can ward off mistakes or any malicious intents of sending conflicting transactions.

Weaknesses:

- **Its blockchain can be much larger.** Because of its fast block generation time, it is capable of processing a high volume of transactions. Unless its network is robust, processing high volumes of transactions can weaken its integrity.

- **Only a few merchants are accepting Litecoin.** While it's similar to the encryption techniques of a popular cryptocurrency (Bitcoin), it's not as widely acceptable as Bitcoin. Litecoins are relatively unknown.

Ripple

Ripple, officially traded as XRP, is another top contender in the cryptocurrency scene. Since its initial launch in 2012, its transactions' need for algorithmic verifications has wowed crowds.

Its design centers on serving as an RTGS (Real-Time Gross Settlement) system. In this system, payment transactions are made in real-time, which means transactions are not subject to a waiting period. Therefore, it is the typical choice for high-value transactions that can benefit from immediate clearing operations.

Strengths:

- **It serves as a bridge currency.** It allows a direct exchange between a pair of currencies at given time. Apart from being freely tradable, its market price is known to fluctuate against USD, JPY, BTC, EUR, and more.

- **It has a grand supply in circulation.** According to CoinMarketCap.com, its supply is more than 39 billion as of February 2018.

- **It is capable of operating on its own.** While Ripple Labs provides heavy back-up, major players support the Ripple network. The supporters include internet service providers and MIT (Massachusetts Institute of Technology).

- **Ripple Labs features an anti-hacking measure.** Whenever you initiate transactions through Ripple's network involving non-native currencies, you will be prompted to pay a fee ranging from $0.000002 (December 2017). This discourages hackers from using the network – unless they're willing to pay transaction fees, which could accumulate to a large sum.

Weaknesses:

- **Its algorithm prevents it from being mined.** A fixed supply of 100 billion XRP tokens were released; the creators (namely Arthur Britto, David Schwartz, and Ryan Fugger) retained 20% of the total supply, and 80% of these tokens were released to Ripple Labs.

Other Promising Cryptocurrencies

Alternative cryptocurrencies or Altcoins are popular digital assets. Altcoins are described to be a cryptocurrency other than Bitcoin. Sure, they're lesser known than Bitcoin, -- and Ethereum, Litecoin, and Ripple -- but their fame is gaining momentum.

A practical reason why you should consider investing in Altcoins is their affordability. If you buy particular Altcoins now, you won't be spending a fortune. If – and this is a huge possibility – the worth of those Altcoins rise significantly in the years to come, you're a wealthy man.

For example, let's look at IOTA. According to CoinMarketCap.com, IOTA's price is $1.57 as of February 2018. If you buy 100 IOTA tokens now, you'll only invest about $150.

Now, if an IOTA token's price reaches $5,000 in 5 years, your $150 investment will become half a million dollars!

Here are some Altcoins worth checking out:

- **Dash**, traded as XCO, is a hybrid cryptocurrency. Its market capitalization peaked at $4.8 billion in 2017. With a major development called Evolution, it automates all transaction-related processes.

   Facts about Dash:

   - Its name is a portmanteau of "digital" and "cash". Its original names were XCoin and DarkCoin.

   - Under the Dark Gravity algorithm, block adjustments are allowed.

   - It features InstandSend, which allows it to confirm transactions fast: at 1.3 seconds.

   - Its Bitcoin code base makes it compatible with Bitcoin-based exchanges, wallets, and other programs.

- **Monero** is traded as XMR with a market capitalization of more than $3 billion (as of February 2018). As an open-source digital asset that was initially released in April 2014, it has established a solid reputation in the industry of cryptocurrencies. Unlike other cryptocurrencies, it is not a derivative of Bitcoin.

   Facts about Monero:

   - It has a virtually infinite supply.

   - Its algorithm features Ring Signatures, which grant absolute privacy to users. It comes with the guarantee that all transactions, despite different points of origin, will land at the same point.

   - Its compatibility with the WordPress Woo-Commerce plugin makes it convenient for the owners of online stores.

   - With the I2P Security Update, it grants anonymity to a user's IP address.

- **Dogecoin**, meant to be a joke, surprised its creator for reaching a market capitalization of $1 billion. Its logo is based on the popular internet meme featuring a version of the face of a Shiba Inu.

   Facts about Dogecoin:

- It invented the craze with tipping services. When a weather forecasting app started to request Dogecoin as tips, other people followed. Eventually, this became a "norm" on sites such as Twitter and Reddit.

- It has a rapid coin production schedule. 100 billion Dogecoins were out in 2015. Years after, it welcomed an additional supply of more than 5 billion. As of February 2018, CoinMarketCap.com reveals its supply in circulation: more than 113 billion.

- **IOTA**, traded as MIOTA, goes past a traditional blockchain. Instead of sticking to the old-fashioned route like other cryptocurrencies, it uses DAG (Direct Acrylic Graph) Technology. Because of this, it doesn't seem too ambitious for considering itself as the next generation blockchain.

  Facts about IOTA:

  - It uses ECC (Elliptic Curve Cryptography), which speeds up transactions with regard to signatures.

  - According to Forrester Research, about 23% of global enterprises are using IOTA and IoT (Internet of Things) solutions.

  - Compared to other cryptocurrencies, it is the winner when it comes to scalability. Its infinite scalability is unparalleled.

  - For IOTA users to make an outgoing transaction, they must first validate a couple of randomly-selections transactions.

- **ADA** is a 3rd-generation digital asset that gives importance to privacy. It is based on a futuristic architecture called RINA (Recursive Inter-Network Architecture). It has a market capitalization of more than $8 billion as of February 2018, as CoinMarketCap.com shows.

  Facts about ADA:

  - It operates on the Cardano blockchain.

  - As it prioritizes a user's privacy, it also aims to allow regulation. While many are against regulation, its objective is to strengthen a network by encouraging participants to follow some ground rules.

  - The development for its own "treasury system" is in the works. This will ensure the sustainability of its protocol.

  - It follows a multi-layer protocol, which solidifies its security for large-scale processes.

- **Stellar** is traded as XLM and is sometimes called Lumens. It is a cryptocurrency and a blockchain project that garners support from a non-profit group called the Stellar Development Foundation. Its initial release was in 2014 with the aim of becoming a global exchange network.

  Facts about Stellar:

  - Its foundation partnered with IBM to accelerate global payments system.

- Its network facilitates cross-asset transactions.

- Its basis was Ripple's protocol. After, it made changes to its consensus code.

Chapter 3 – How to Buy Cryptocurrencies

Before using your hard-earned money to buy (or even hoard) cryptocurrencies, you have to decide on a particular cryptocurrency. Buying random cryptocurrencies is a bad call, and the same is true when investing in assets with limited interest.

It's important to familiarize yourself with the cryptocurrency you're about to buy since you'll be watching its progress on financial markets. You'll need to monitor relevant news and record price fluctuations, recent market price, impact on global economics, market value, and other important details about it.

So do you believe in Bitcoin and Ethereum's growth potential? How about the potential in Litecoin, Ripple, and other Altcoins? Or do you prefer to buy a single cryptocurrency (for example, just Bitcoin)?

Once you've decided, you can officially begin!

Step 1: Open a Cryptocurrency Wallet

First, open a cryptocurrency wallet. Owning a cryptocurrency wallet grants you the authority to send, receive, and manage cryptocurrencies.

Types of cryptocurrency wallets:

- **Mobile wallets**. Those who do not own PCs and those who are often on-the-go prefer these wallets. Their major plus is the easy accessibility of cryptographic keys (both public and private).
  - Most mobile wallets also allow links to desktop and web-based functions.
- **Desktop wallets.** A benefit of these wallets is the support they offer for multiple cryptocurrencies.
  - Examples of desktop wallets:
    - Coinbase (Bitcoin, Litecoin, and Ethereum only)
    - Mobi (Bitcoin only)
    - Electrum (Bitcoin only)
    - Coinomi
- **Hardware wallets.** Apart from supporting multiple cryptocurrencies, another advantage of these wallets is that they are not hackable online.
  - Examples of hardware wallets:
    - Trezor
    - Ledger Nano S
    - OpenDime (Bitcoin only)
    - KeepKey

- **Paper wallets.** Ideally, these wallets are great for "old school" investors. Such wallets won't threaten long-term security. So if you're planning to store cryptocurrencies for years, they're a great choice. And since their natures isn't reliant on a digital presence, they're not prone to computer-related damages.

    o You can easily create a paper wallet by printing a wallet address from a trusted online wallet generator. Once you have a print, secure it so nobody can access it.

- **Web-based wallets.** These wallets are linkable to mobile and desktop wallets. And since they function via the internet, the storage of private keys is secured online.

    o Examples of web-based wallets:

        - GreenAddress (Bitcoin only)

        - Xapo (Bitcoin only)

        - CoinVault

        - Coin.Space (Bitcoin and Litecoin only)

Hot Storage vs. Cold Storage: Which Is the Better Choice?

On the subject of cryptocurrency wallets, it's likely you'll encounter the terms "hot storage" and "cold storage".

Hot storage refers to cryptocurrency storage via the internet. Examples are the storage of your coins via a web-based wallet.

The main upside of this system is the *allowance of immediate withdrawals*. So if you want to buy cryptocurrencies that you'll later withdraw, you should opt for this system. Granted you only buy a small amount of cryptocurrencies, you have the prerogative to cash them into traditional currency almost instantly. For this, you wouldn't have to wait about a week for the completion of a transaction.

You can also store and withdraw large amounts of cryptocurrencies if you go with this storage system. But be advised that it's not recommended.

And if you withdraw large amounts, you can't usually get the amount instantly. As a safety measure, the party in charge of the withdrawals limits the cryptocurrencies in hot storage. Therefore, there is a delay in the withdrawal process since retrieving the cryptocurrencies from another storage system is necessary.

The safer storage system is cold storage. This system refers to *cryptocurrency storage via offline means*. If you own a large amount of cryptocurrencies and don't have a need for immediate withdrawals, it's your best bet.

Here are some cold storage methods:

- Using paper wallets

- Using safety deposit boxes and USB drives

- Using offline hardware wallets

- Using bearer instruments such as Bitbill and Casascius physical bitcoin (for Bitcoin)

The downside to cold storage is that this system is costly. Usually, you need a minimum of $80 to afford a cold storage system.

Computer Storage Is Not Always a Good Idea

You may also think of your computer as a storage system for your cryptocurrencies. Indeed, it's possible to store the public and private keys of your wallet on a computer. But while it can work, this arrangement is not recommended.

Here are reasons why you shouldn't rely on computers as cryptocurrency storage systems:

- Computers come with the possibility of crashing. They can get burned or smoke-damaged, too. Therefore, you need a good data recovery system in case this happens.

- Computers can be broken into without authorization. If a hacker knows your physical address, they can sneak into your home and access your computer.

- Powerful magnetic fields can corrupt data on a traditional HDD (Hard Disc Drive).

- Unpowered SSDs (Solid State Drives) can result in data loss if unused for years. They are not meant for long-term cryptocurrency storage.

- Computers are susceptible to ongoing threats. They are at risk against 0-day exploits, malicious USB cords, and firmware exploits.

Step 2: Buy Cryptocurrencies

After opening a cryptocurrency wallet, you'll be assigned public and private cryptographic key. The public key can be shared. The private key, on the other hand, is not.

Here is an example of a private cryptographic key:

```
1GyKzZu78tUN7HsYRJWV1w6zKhdnPPpwht
```

Remember this cryptographic key since you'll need to send incoming cryptocurrency purchases to it.

From Cryptocurrency Exchanges

Now, go to a cryptocurrency exchange. It's one of the simplest ways. It can be a trading platform, direct person-to-person trading, or broker. All these types of exchanges can allow you to buy cryptocurrencies.

Popular cryptocurrency exchanges are GDAX, Bittrex, Poloniex, Kraken, and Cryptopia. As a first-timer, it's advisable to avail of the services of these exchanges since they have very straightforward systems. They have established websites where you can find answers to common questions. Additionally, there are plenty of tutorials about how to use them online.

Once you've decided on an exchange, head to its website. On the website of a cryptocurrency exchange, register for an account. Fill in the right information and personal details, and follow these steps:

1. First, go to the trade section on GDAX and choose **BTC-USD**. On the upper left, click **Deposit** to the deposit an amount in USD.

2. Once you've made a successful deposit, trade USD for BTC. This will reflect on your account.

3. Once you have BTC in your GDAX account, navigate to the trade section. Then, choose **Withdraw**.

4. Finally, withdraw all the BTC in your GDAX account to your cryptocurrency. In this process, you'll need to input your wallet address.

*This is based on a BTC-USD transaction via GDAX. Note that you can also buy other cryptocurrencies or use other traditional currencies as payment on GDAX. Likewise, you can also use other cryptocurrency exchanges.

And in some cases, a cryptocurrency wallet also extends its services to buying and selling cryptocurrencies. An example is Coinbase. If you own a Coinbase wallet, you can fund it directly with cryptocurrencies.

1. Login to your Coinbase account. Then go to the **Buy/Sell** section.

2. Next, click the **Buy** tab. The Buy tab is the Buy/Sell section's default tab. But you should double-check.

3. Next, select your wallet from the **Deposit from** dropdown menu. Then enter the amount of Bitcoins you want to buy.

4. Finalize the transaction.

One vs. Two & More Cryptocurrency Purchase

If you're a beginner, it's advisable to start with a single cryptocurrency. This lets you avoid confusion from having to interpret multiple data. With a lot of cryptocurrencies on your plate, you can feel overwhelmed by the responsibility, too.

And it's also best for this cryptocurrency to be Bitcoin. Due to Bitcoin's popularity, you have more opportunities to use it. Remember, most wallets and exchanges are Bitcoin-friendly.

Understand how Bitcoin works and commit to learning its strengths and weaknesses. It's important to focus on a single cryptocurrency at this point because this will serve as your foundation for future cryptocurrency investments.

Once you're ready, that's when you consider exploring other cryptocurrencies. If you don't think your initial cryptocurrency investment is the right choice for you, you can sell it as a means of capital for other cryptocurrencies.

Storing Cryptocurrencies

Buying cryptocurrencies is a start – and only that. Remember, being financially-capable of buying cryptocurrencies is a privilege. And unless you maximize this privilege, you'll only regret buying cryptocurrencies.

Basic Protection

A basic way to maximize this privilege is to safeguard your cryptocurrencies. Always be careful and take extra steps since online security is critical when you're dealing with digital assets. As a cryptocurrency owner, think twice before clicking links and downloading e-mail attachments.

Cryptocurrencies may be vulnerable to the hacking efforts of proficient hacking groups. Therefore, you should do your part by following security measures. In fact, it's advisable that those with limited knowledge on cybersecurity shouldn't own cryptocurrencies.

Here are some tips:

- **Transfer cryptocurrencies from an exchange to a wallet.** Don't store the coins in an exchange. Then treat the wallet as if it were your credit card.

  There is a pressing concern that exchanges have a relatively inferior ability to safeguard user data and a user's cryptocurrencies. They're also known to go down occasionally. Securing your cryptocurrencies, after all, is not their priority.

- **Use 2FA (Two-Factor Authentication).** In normal instances such as checking Facebook, 2FA is a time-consuming process since it mandates you to verify your identity even after you already provided login details. Entering your username and password is only the first step. If you can't enter a code that was sent to you via e-mail or SMS, entry is invalid.

  But since the ownership of cryptocurrencies doesn't fall in the "normal instances" category, you should use 2FA. It greatly increases security since the verification process involves the input of private personal information (i.e. information that only you know).

- **Be wise when connecting to Wi-Fi networks.** As much as possible, don't connect to public Wi-Fi networks using a device with your cryptocurrency wallet on it. Establish a connection only with a network of trustworthy people.

  Similarly, avoid visiting high-risk websites (i.e. a non-HTTPS site or any site that an antivirus tags as such) or leave your device unattended.

- **Be careful of phishing sites.** Unfortunately, the number of phishing websites that ask for your private wallet key is increasing – and their targets are cryptocurrency owners. So always be vigilant and only enter your private wallet key on a trusted and authoritative site.

- **Transfer your wallet from a device that needs repair.** If you need a service provider to check your PC, make sure that your cryptocurrency wallet is no longer on that PC. Temporarily transfer it instead to another storage system such as a mobile-based wallet.

On a related note, prioritize the need to change wallets regularly. This lets you avoid threats to your account's security. Security, after all, could thin over time.

- **Have a separate wallet for "spending" and for "investments".** It's not preferable to have a "universal" storage system for all your cryptocurrencies. Instead, compartmentalize.

  While it offers the convenience of not having more than one wallet to worry about, this arrangement is also likely to result in confusion. This introduces the possibility of using your cryptocurrency investments for luxury spending.

Going Another Mile

Now, if you own millions of cryptocurrencies, you need to go the extra mile with regard to security. A Forbes report reveals that the number of people who hack into cryptocurrency wallets is increasing. And as the years continue, these hackers are getting better at these illegal activities.

While it is advantageous, the privacy of using cryptocurrencies can also backfire on you. If cryptocurrencies slip from your possession, most likely, they're gone forever. And unfortunately, retrieval of these lost assets is quite impossible.

- **Don't use mobile wallets in this case.** The user-friendliness of mobile wallets go both ways: they're user-friendly for cryptocurrency owners and hackers. So reserve them for storing small amounts of cryptocurrencies, preferably less than $100 worth of these coins.

- **Leverage the use of Google Authenticator's IP whitelist feature.** Enable only a single IP for account verification with Google Authenticator. It's advisable to enable just yours and access your wallet from a single device.

- **Don't undermine the importance of a great backup system.** Start with one external hard drive or a flash drive to back-up the files that contain your public and private cryptographic keys. Then go with a 2nd and a 3rd one. This safeguards your wallet in case your device is rendered unusable.

  Software and hardware may be important, but they are replaceable. Your files that contain your wallet address, on the other hand, are not.

- **Don't undermine the importance of encryption**. It's a must to encrypt sensitive data. Therefore, it's a must to encrypt your public and private cryptographic keys. Recommended encryption services for this case are VeraCrypt, Serpent, and Twofish.

- **Sign up for an anti-virus program's premium subscription**. Free subscriptions are good – excellent, even – at identifying malicious files. The catch is that these free services equate to your data being sold as a monetization strategy.

  So since you can afford to hoard a lot of cryptocurrencies, it's likely you can afford a premium anti-virus program, too. Some recommended anti-virus programs are Kapersky, BitDefender, and Eset Internet Security.

- **Diversify your risks.** Do not store all your cryptocurrencies in a single wallet. If all your security measures fail, you have other wallets to turn to.

Chapter 4 - How to Trade Cryptocurrencies

As you finish funding your cryptocurrency wallet, it's time to take matters up a notch by trading cryptocurrencies on financial markets. Cryptocurrency trading is similar to forex trading; the main difference is that instead of trading USD, JPY, GBP, and other traditional currencies against other traditional currencies as a forex trader, you'll be trading cryptocurrencies against traditional currencies or other cryptocurrencies as a cryptocurrency trader.

You may get started simply by heading to a trading platform and trade away. Just make sure you keep some notes in mind.

How to Choose the Right Trading Platform

Most – if not all – trading platforms for cryptocurrency trading require a minimum deposit. The amount varies; some ask for $20 while others want big amounts such as $250.

It's good if you can afford the minimum deposit. But look past this "qualification" and focus on other areas of a trading platform.

- **Review the allowable leverage.** Especially if you're starting with limited funds, a trading platform's allowable leverage plays a vital role in your future trading activities. Allowable leverage means that you are allowed to execute trades beyond an initial deposit.

  So choose a platform that allows high leverage. A 2:1 leverage ratio is available. You should go for this ratio (or a ratio like it). 2:1 leverage means the margin requirement (minimum) is 1/2 or 50%. This also means that you are allowed to secure a trade that is twice as valuable as your current trading account.

- **Determine the allowable cryptocurrencies and currencies.** Not all trading platforms for cryptocurrency trading allows the execution of trades involving all types of cryptocurrencies.

  Usually, most – if not all – cryptocurrency exchanges accept trade executions for Bitcoin, Ethereum, Litecoin, and Ripple. Conversely, the less popular Altcoins such as Dash, IOTA, Monero, IOTA, ADA, and Stellar are not allowable on many cryptocurrency exchanges.

- **Make sure it allows important trading features.** Trading features such as real-time price charts, hedging, placement of stop losses, access to corporate data, and proper automation functions grant better control over your cryptocurrency tokens and trades. Consider using a trading platform that allows them.

  Then again, only consider this if these features can improve the quality of your trades. If you won't be relying on them, these trading features are unnecessary.

- **Familiarize yourself with all the fees.** Don't trade blindly by not taking into account transaction fees. And be informed of any hidden fee.

  Transparency is important since you can only determine actual profitability once you've deducted all the applicable fees. It's your responsibility to know any service charges for each trade. And it should be a trading platform's responsibility to disclose all the charges to you.

- **Choose a platform that allows multi-channel accessibility.** Many traders prefer to receive updates about their trading activities on their mobile devices. Some of them even want to execute trades via these devices. This way, even if they live active lifestyles, they can keep up with their trades.

    If you, yourself, are always on-the-go, choose a trading platform with multi-channel accessibility. Look beyond web-based trading platforms. Make sure that your choice of trading platform comes with an app that you can easily use on your mobile devices.

Recommended Platforms for Cryptocurrency Trading

Mentioned above are factors to consider when choosing a platform for cryptocurrency trading. Now, here are some platforms that qualify according to the checklist.

Cryptofy.me (for GDAX Account)

Many people are impressed at the seamlessness of their GDAX accounts. Traders of all levels turn to GDAX, and the more experienced ones prefer it over other platforms due to its topnotch security and community trust. It also offers very low transaction fees and good customer support.

That said, there's Cryptofy.me. It is a downloadable trading platform for GDAX users. While it's not the official GDAX app, its servers are located in similar data centers as the servers of GDAX. Therefore, minimal latency can be provided.

It provides important information that a GDAX account reflects. This includes custom price notifications, order management, and price spike notifications.

Instructions:

1. First, open Cryptofy.me. Then, connect it to your GDAX account.

2. Next, download the GDAX API Key. Then, set it up.

3. Start trading.

Coinbase

Then, there's Coinbase. In Chapter 3, you can find instructions on how to buy cryptocurrencies from Coinbase. You can review the same instructions since they are also applicable as trading instructions.

Coinbase is the top Bitcoin startup. It has garnered funds since it encourages trading activities with a set price -- and market value as the basis. Not only are the prices of cryptocurrencies fairly reasonable, this arrangement also allows faster purchases.

Coinbase charges lower fees: no more than $3.99 (as of January 2018). For those with large trading orders, the low fees are definitely a plus.

Other than bank transfers, credit card payments are also allowed in Coinbase. This is a striking feature since not many platforms have flexible payment methods. With Coinbase, granted you can provide your full name, e-mail, and credit card verification, you're fit for trading.

TabTrader (for Accounts on Popular Exchanges)

If you have existing accounts on web-based cryptocurrency exchanges, consider using the TabTrader platform. It supports Coinbase, Poloniex, Bitfinex, BitMarket, Kraken, Clevercoin, Cryptsy, and a lot more. So if your exchange is good, despite the unavailability of a mobile app, consider maintaining your account on that exchange, and just download TabTrader to make your account mobile-friendly.

Apart from offering support for multiple cryptocurrency exchanges, the winning TabTrader features are as follows:

- Margin trading support

- Chart trading capabilities

- API keys (exchange) encryption

- PIN protection

- Order book

Best of all, TabTrader is 100% free. This is a big upside considering how other programs charge monthly fees. It doesn't feature ads or ask to complete a survey.

Instructions:

1. First, download TabTrader. Then connect your account on a cryptocurrency exchange.

2. Next, download the API key of your cryptocurrency exchange. Then set it up and make sure to allow permissions to sell, buy, and view balance.

3. Trade away.

ShapeShift

ShapeShift is an advisable choice if you're looking for a trading platform that processes transactions instantly. It lets you instantly convert cryptocurrencies into traditional currencies or into other cryptocurrencies.

An upside is its support for more than 50 cryptocurrencies. This includes Bitcoin, Ethereum, Litecoin, Ripple, and Dash.

Additionally, it has a beginner-friendly website and mobile app. So if you're new to cryptocurrencies, consider this option.

Instructions:

1. First, download the ShapeShift mobile app.

2. Next, register for an account.

3. Start trading.

Decentralized Exchanges

You can also trade cryptocurrencies on a decentralized exchange. An advantage of this is the same advantage when using cryptocurrencies: total privacy.

A decentralized exchange doesn't rely on 3rd party services to hold funds. Instead, it allows trades to proceed directly – from one peer to another peer. To trade cryptocurrencies with another person, you'll be the one to process all of the transaction requirements.

Basically, you're on your own. On a decentralized exchange, there are no useful features such as margin trading and stop loss placements. To maximize your profitability for your trades, you need to use other resources from other websites.

If you decide to use a decentralized exchange, having experienced trading on a centralized cryptocurrency exchange is advisable.

Here are some recommended decentralized exchanges:

Waves Dex

Waves Dex, engineered on the blockchain called Waves, is a decentralized exchange that grants you total control of your funds. Then it accelerates exchange processes by relying on a centralized exchange.

With Waves Dex, you are free to trade cryptocurrencies in exchange for an asset issued on the platform. As of 2018, the exchange offers 72 assets at 182 BTC.

Start using the exchange simply by completing a registration form. A tip is to safeguard your registration's back phrase since this back phrase can help with the restoration of your funds.

CryptoBridge Dex

If you're familiar with the BitShares network, you might want to familiarize yourself with CryptoBridge Dex, too. It is on this network that CryptoBridge Dex operates. The volume is 201 BTC, and there are 32 issuable assets.

A great aspect of CryptoBridge Dex is its support for decentralized trading without even a single point of failure. You can even trade all the most popular Altcoin pairs such as Dash and IOTA. On top of that, you are the only one who can access your funds.

Stellar Dex

Other than just a cryptocurrency and a blockchain project, Stellar has a native decentralized exchange. Having a native exchange makes it very convenient. This is a major reason why owners of the Stellar cryptocurrency use this exchange.

To begin using Stellar Dex, just head to the Stellar Dex website. There, you'll need to create an account by generating a key pair. One pair is a public key and the other is a secret key.

Once you create a key pair, you can login to your account. You can start trading after you make a deposit of 20 lumens.

A setback is that there are only 6 issuable assets on the Stellar network. As of 2018, the volume is 36 BTC.

DOs & DON'Ts as a Cryptocurrency Trader

Once you've chosen a trading platform, you can let your trading activities commence. Remember to trade wisely, of course. Discern what you need to do and what you shouldn't do, rather than feel overconfident.

Just like forex trading, cryptocurrency trading is highly-risky. If you're not careful, you could lose big during your first time.

List of DOs:

- **Decide and stand by your decision.** f you decide to buy a cryptocurrency, be absolutely sure that you want to bet on it. Don't buy it for shallow reasons such as "because my friend bought it too". Instead, buy it because you bel eve in its growth potential. Buy it because it can maximize your profitability.

  The same goes if you decide to sell a cryptocurrency. Don't just sell it for the wrong reasons such as "because Warren Buffett doesn't want anything g to do with it anymore".

  Decide whether you buy and/or sell and then get it over with. Fickle-mindedness is not a good friend to have in this case. It can only drain you of energy and cloud your judgment. If a trade is not favorable on your end, move on.

- **Take profits often when you're dealing with Altcoins.** Altcoins have great growth potential. But while this is true, you have to note that their potential is much lower compared to those of the major cryptocurrencies.

  Let's review data from CoinMarketCap.com involving a major cryptocurrency, Ethereum, and an Altcoin, Stellar. As of February 2018, Ethereum's price is on the $770 mark. Stellar's price, on the other hand, is less than $1.

  So if you get a profit of about $20 for your Altcoin investment, you should already consider it a win. For all you know, this $20 profit could reverse to a negative $20 in just a couple of hours.

- **Be willing to go big.** Many of the world's successful investors (including George Soros) stick to this advice. Trading big with cryptocurrencies means you should be willing to go all in on a trade and stomach its carried risks. Trading halfheartedly is dissatisfying and can exhaust you sooner or later.

  On the other hand, learn to have a safety zone, too. Take risks – calculated ones. Always prepare for the worst case scenario because trading can introduce you to such a scenario. For example, don't trade all your life savings for cryptocurrencies.

  It's wise to go big on your trades, but only if you can afford it. While there's a possibility of winning big if you go big, there's also a possibility of losing big if you go big.

- **Get news from trustworthy reporters.** Being updated with the latest happenings on your cryptocurrency investments makes for better management and higher chances of profitability. Past and current market prices, historical records, global reach, and latest notable investors are examples of the important news that you should monitor.

  But while getting news is important, getting news from the right sources is more important. An unfortunate fact is that the number of false news about cryptocurrencies is increasing. If you're gullible and end up getting information from these fake sites, you're unlikely to succeed as a cryptocurrency investor.

List of DON'Ts:

- **Beware of the Classic "Pump and Dump" Scheme.** Amateur cryptocurrency investors fall prey to this corrupt approach that involves hype on social media. In this approach, cryptocurrencies are "pumped"; a bogus entity uses false positive claims, success stories, and other attractive statements to promote these cryptocurrencies. Once a pre-determined limit is reached, this bogus entity gets notified to start the "dump"; he'll begin selling off.

  If a new cryptocurrency is released, it's not a wise idea to buy it on the spot. A solution is to look beyond the hype and look beyond momentary gains. Only invest in cryptocurrencies that have proven themselves to be solid digital assets.

- **Don't panic-sell.** If you hear news that the price of a cryptocurrency you invested in is going down, keep it cool. Give it a day (or weeks or months), and then you'll probably see a return in a peak price.

  Don't panic by selling all of your tokens. Remember, cryptocurrencies are highly-volatile investments. Take Ripple, for example. Its price once soared by 64% in less than a day.

  Conversely, avoid letting excitement get the better of you. If you hear news that the price of a cryptocurrency will keep going up, it's not best to start hoarding a supply.

- **Avoid compulsive trading.** Instead, always have a brilliant strategy in place and be rational. Allowing recent market positions to dictate your trading activity can be disastrous.

  Even forex traders are discouraged from trading compulsively. Traders of cryptocurrencies are highly-advised not to engage in this kind of trading considering cryptocurrency charts tend to move faster than forex charts.

Chapter 5 – Tips on Managing Cryptocurrency Investments

Cryptocurrency investments are highly-speculative. Their chances of significant profits are proportional to chances of significant losses. So there's a possibility of you profiting a lot, but there's also a possibility of you losing disastrously.

If you're aware of this, then go ahead and pursue cryptocurrencies.

Sure, the Winklevoss twins, Tim Draper, Charlie Shrem, Barry Silbert, and many other people are bathing in fortune because of these digital assets.

But other people (Warren Buffett, to name one) are hesitant. According to them, cryptocurrencies are flying high only because they're inside a bubble. The time will come that this bubble will pop and all of the value with it will plummet.

If these doubters are right -- if the bubble does pop soon -- it looks like you're doomed. Or are you? If you're a brilliant strategist who knows how to manage this type of investments, you're probably going to be okay.

Now Is the Best Time to Buy Cryptocurrencies

Financial analysts (including CNBC fast trader, Brian Kelly) say *now is the best time to buy cryptocurrencies*. Behind this analogy is the classic statement:

> *"The best time to plant a tree was 10 years ago.*
>
> *The second best time to do so is now."*

Technically, the best time was years ago when cryptocurrencies hit the market. But even if you beat yourself up as many times as you wish, you can't go back in time.

Bitcoin, for example, was first traded for a couple of pizza slices. 10,000 BTC, to be exact, for two slices of pizza. If only the then-Bitcoin owner zeroed in on Bitcoin's price of (about) $10,000 in 2018, there probably wouldn't have been a trade.

Financial analysts would reference to such tale to make a point. According to them, the massive growth potential of cryptocurrencies shouldn't be ignored.

Let's review the price increase in major cryptocurrencies:

- Bitcoin's price is now up to 5 figures. It's going to reach the million dollar mark, according to predictions.

- Ethereum is up by 2,800%.

- Litecoin has gone from $100 (November 2017) to $300 (December 2017)

- Ripple's price grew by 64% in just 17 hours in December 2017

These financial analysts are also addressing the intimidating nature of cryptocurrencies in this area. Arguably, the concept of cryptocurrencies can be frightening to most people for some of the following reasons:

- They have no idea how the blockchain technology works

- They are anxious of opening a cryptocurrency wallet

- They are unfamiliar with how exchanges work

- The process of buying cryptocurrencies seems to take a lot of work

And instead of overcoming their fright, they would rather pass up the opportunity to buy cryptocurrencies.

If you view matters from an outsider's perspective, you should realize that this (i.e. the fact that most people are hesitant to make cryptocurrency investments) is favorable to you. This means cryptocurrencies are yet to be mainstream, which is a reason to start investing now.

More importantly, the opportunity to jump on the bandwagon earlier means you're given an edge over them: experience and potential gain. Sooner or later, these once hesitant bunch is likely to jump on the bandwagon, too.

Using Cryptocurrency Trackers

As you build your portfolio, you should continually track your cryptocurrencies. Doing so allows you to be updated with price and market changes and useful information about your cryptocurrencies. It also allows you to visualize profits and losses.

One way to keep track of a particular cryptocurrency is to visit its website daily. But if you need to track multiple cryptocurrencies, this is a very tedious and time-consuming process.

The better way is to download cryptocurrency tracking apps on your mobile device. These programs are built to deliver the latest news on multiple cryptocurrencies. With them, all you have to do is check your mobile device.

Some of the recommended cryptocurrency tracking app are as follows:

CoinTelegraph

CoinTelegraph supports Bitcoin and Ethereum only apart from news about finance and the blockchain technology. With the app, you can categorize news according to "Hottest" and "Latest". It also encourages the distribution of news to social networking sites.

Blockfolio

If you want to go beyond Bitcoin and Ethereum, Blockfolio makes a great choice. It supports not one, two, or ten cryptocurrencies, but 800 cryptocurrencies! It supports Bitcoin, Ethereum, Litecoin, Ripple, Monero, Dash, IOTA, ADA, Dogecoin, Stellar, and more.

A key feature is its "Portfolio Overview" function. This lets you see a list of all your cryptocurrencies, which are all easily clickable to get detailed news.

It also comes with a "Price Notification" function. This function gives you the prerogative of receiving notifications as soon as the price of a cryptocurrency cross a pre-determined threshold.

Zupcoin Bot

Then there's Zupcoin Bot. It's not an app, but rather a chat bot that can serve as your personal assistant with regard to price inquiries about a cryptocurrency pair on a particular trading platform or exchange.

For example, you want to know the price of Ethereum to USD on GDAX. To start, launch Zupcoin Bot and on the message box, type the keywords "ETH to USD on GDAX".

CoinDesk

If you're after instant news, CoinDesk is suggested for you. It lets you access news instantly, together with calculators, graphs, and price charts. You can get it for Android and iOS phones.

CoinPaper

CoinPaper gives you the live price of a cryptocurrency on your mobile's wallpaper. Since it uses an API, it's highly customizable. This means you are free to choose the background, colors, coins, and more.

Short-Term vs. Long-Term Investing

Whether you're in it for short-term or for long-term gains, you can profit as a cryptocurrency investor. It's important to define and understand how you're handling cryptocurrencies. Know the set of advantages and disadvantages of your approach for it to work in your favor.

You can invest in any coin you like. Litecoin, Ripple, and other Altcoins make perfect short-term investment vehicles. These cryptocurrencies pose less risk of losses. Meanwhile, the major players for long-term investing are Bitcoin and Ethereum. As historical records can attest, these digital assets have significantly boosted the portfolio value of long-term investors.

Short Term

You're a short-term investor if you buy cryptocurrencies, hold them for a short or medium waiting period, and then sell them for profit. You're investing for a relatively short period: minutes, days, weeks, or months.

A major advantage of short-term investing is the ability to seize the opportunity for immediate high percentage gains. If the price of a cryptocurrency suddenly increases, you can take advantage of it. you can buy (or sell) it right then and there.

For example, there's Bitcoin's $9,600 price that rose to $10,000 on November 27, 2017. So if you're a short-term investor who bought 5 Bitcoins worth $9,600 apiece (totaling $48,000), you can sell all those 5 Bitcoins for $50,000. Consequently, you would've gained $2,000 in the process – within a 24-hour timeframe.

A setback of this approach is the stress involved. You need to keep an eye on the market and when the time calls for it, decide if you should sell or keep the tokens in your possession.

Short-term investing is ideal for you if you have these qualities:

- Confidence in your technical analysis skills

- Excellent decision-making skills

- Financial capability of using decent capital to generate gains (sizable) from percentage movements

- A need (and preference) for immediate returns

- Time for consistent analysis and a watchful eye for market movements

Long Term

Then, there's long-term investing. Many financially-skilled people refer to it as "hodling", *the Cold Storage Trading Strategy*, and *Buy and Hold*. This strategy is preferred by the more passive cryptocurrency investors who are very patient in seeing a cryptocurrency's progress through the years.

Such approach involves three steps:

1. First, you buy a supply of cryptocurrency tokens.

2. Next, you store the supply in a paper wallet. Then you wait for a long period (at least two years).

3. Finally, sell/trade it for another cryptocurrency or currency.

Its advantage over short-term investing is its virtually effortless execution. It doesn't open opportunities for stress over sudden price movements. It doesn't even require you to be excellent at technical analysis. All you need to do is wait for some time to pass. By then, there's a big possibility that you'll be profiting a lot.

Let's use 5 Bitcoin tokens as an example once more. If you invested in Bitcoin in June 2013, you'd be cashing in $500 (1 Bitcoin = $100 in June 2013) for 5 Bitcoins. If you let it sit until January 2018, you can sell those 5 Bitcoin tokens for about $50,000 (1 Bitcoin = $10,000 in January 2018). Now, that's a profit of $49,500 in almost 5 years' time.

If you like the example, you'll like the idea of long-term investing, too. Here are some reasons why long-term investing is suited for you if:

- You're not exactly a skilled investor. You want to have an investment that only requires easy and simple upkeep.

- You lack time and motivation for active investing.

The Importance of Diversification

As an investor, you should also think about diversification. For an apparent reason, diversifying your investment portfolio significantly reduces your losses. If the value of one cryptocurrency seems to be going down, it shouldn't bother you too much since you have another cryptocurrency that can compensate for the probable loss.

A tip is to fill your portfolio with a combination of low-risk and high-risk cryptocurrencies. For example, buy Bitcoin, Ethereum, Monero, and Dash for a healthy investment portfolio.

Due to their multi-billion market capitalizations, Bitcoin and Ethereum are relatively low-risk options. Monero and Dash are examples of high-risk cryptocurrencies since they have lower market capitalization.

Examples

Here's an example of a scenario in which you have diversified your investment portfolio. You have 40 tokens in your wallet: 10 ETH, 10 BTC, 10 LTC, and 10 XRP. Hypothetically, if Ethereum goes downhill, you won't necessarily be going downhill. In the same hypothetical scenario, you also have Bitcoin, Litecoin, and Ripple, which are all rising. You'll have 10 tokens that are depreciating and 30 tokens that are all appreciating.

Now, here's an example of a scenario in which you haven't diversified your investment portfolio. Hypothetically, you only bought Ethereum tokens; you have 40 ETH. If Ethereum goes down, it looks like you (and your 40 tokens) are going down and no other cryptocurrency can compensate for your loss.

Additional Reasons

Portfolio diversification is also important since it can make the waiting period worthwhile. If one of your main cryptocurrency investments is not giving returns, you should stop obsessing over it and instead, invest in another cryptocurrency during the process.

Buying other cryptocurrency options and leaving your main cryptocurrency investment be is a strategic approach. It eliminates opportunities for making panic-based decisions and impulsive exchanges.

Experience is another part of the deal if you diversify your investment portfolio. Investing in a cryptocurrency lets you gain knowledge about that type of cryptocurrency. You'll learn important information such as:

- Volatility

- Price growth

- Particular news' (e.g. new investors and social media promotions) impact on it

Then, you can compare these information on a particular cryptocurrency to information about other cryptocurrencies. From this point, you'll understand which cryptocurrencies are favorable to you and which ones aren't.

Selective Diversification

On the other hand, only diversify your investment portfolio with familiar cryptocurrencies – or those that you're interested in learning about. Don't just buy particular types of cryptocurrencies for the sake of diversifying. If you're unwilling to do your research, it's best to eliminate that cryptocurrency in your portfolio.

For example, you want to have your cryptocurrencies in your portfolio other than Bitcoin. So you buy Ethereum and Ripple. Afterwards, your responsibility is to research important information about Ethereum and Ripple. So you determine useful details such as their market capitalization, price fluctuations, and economic impact.

Conclusion

Thanks for downloading this book, **Cryptocurrency Investing Guide: How To Make A Lot Of Money By Investing in Bitcoin, Ethereum, Litecoin & Ripple**. I hope you've learned the nature of cryptocurrencies, how cryptocurrencies work, and how you can buy and trade your own cryptocurrencies. I also hope you've learned important management tips

After coursing through this 5-chapter book, I hope you learned enough to confidently start your journey as a cryptocurrency investor.

Sure, the concept of cryptocurrencies may be a bit complex. But cryptocurrencies can lead you to your own empire. Just remember to work hard. Use the step-by-step tutorials and tips from this book to help you.

Other than that, do not hold back from investing resources. And this not only includes money and effort, but also time. After sacrificing your time so you could learn the ropes, it might not be long until you reap much-deserved rewards.

Most importantly, always stay focused on your end goal of making a lot of money with these cryptocurrencies. Don't let minor inconveniences such as unexpected price changes throw you off your game. The volatility of cryptocurrencies is usually soaring, so there's a possibility of you experiencing losses.

You may even encounter some people whose doubts on cryptocurrencies can discourage you. In such cases, remember that not everyone share similar opinions. Better yet, don't pay attention to them and instead, wow them with promising results.

Good Luck!

Made in the USA
Las Vegas, NV
23 October 2021